ALL-TIME
POPULAR SONGS
FOR VIOLIN DUET

ISBN 978-1-4950-9005-9

HAL•LEONARD®

7777 W. BLUEMOUND RD. P.O. BOX 13819 MILWAUKEE, WI 53213

Visit Hal Leonard Online at
www.halleonard.com

BILLIE JEAN

Words and Music by
MICHAEL JACKSON

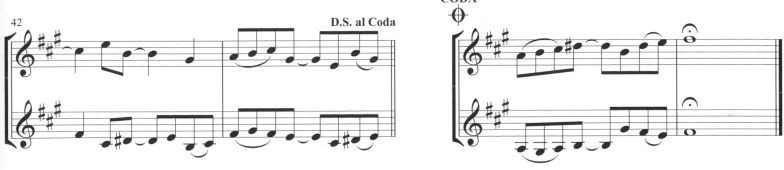

BOHEMIAN RHAPSODY

VIOLIN

Words and Music by
FREDDIE MERCURY

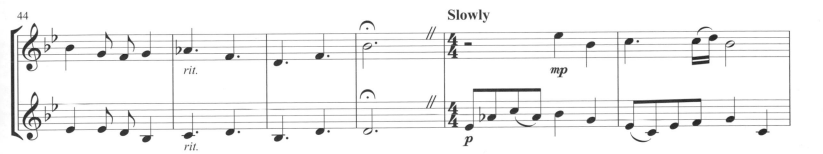

BRIDGE OVER TROUBLED WATER

VIOLIN

Words and Music by
PAUL SIMON

Moderately

To Coda

D.S. al Coda

CODA

CALIFORNIA DREAMIN'

VIOLIN

Words and Music by JOHN PHILLIPS
and MICHELLE PHILLIPS

Medium Rock

D.S. al Coda

CODA

CAN YOU FEEL THE LOVE TONIGHT

from THE LION KING

VIOLIN

Music by ELTON JOHN
Lyrics by TIM RICE

CAN'T HELP FALLING IN LOVE

VIOLIN

Words and Music by GEORGE DAVID WEISS,
HUGO PERETTI and LUIGI CREATORE

Moderately slow

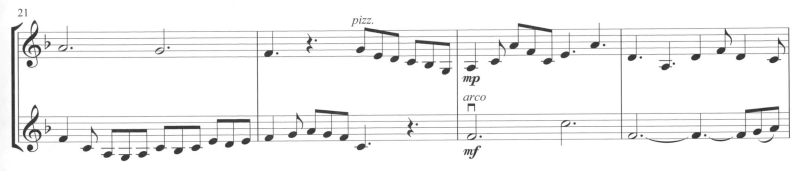

EVERY BREATH YOU TAKE

VIOLIN

Music and Lyrics by
STING

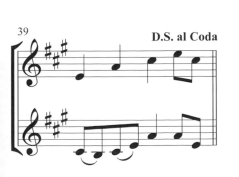

GOOD VIBRATIONS

VIOLIN

Words and Music by BRIAN WILSON
and MIKE LOVE

HALLELUJAH

VIOLIN

Words and Music by
LEONARD COHEN

Moderately slow

I HEARD IT THROUGH THE GRAPEVINE

VIOLIN

Words and Music by NORMAN J. WHITFIELD
and BARRETT STRONG

I WILL ALWAYS LOVE YOU

VIOLIN

Words and Music by
DOLLY PARTON

IMAGINE

VIOLIN

Words and Music by
JOHN LENNON

Slowly

IN MY LIFE

VIOLIN

Words and Music by JOHN LENNON
and PAUL McCARTNEY

Moderately

LEAN ON ME

VIOLIN

Words and Music by
BILL WITHERS

Moderately slow

MOON RIVER

from the Paramount Picture BREAKFAST AT TIFFANY'S

VIOLIN

Words by JOHNNY MERCER
Music by HENRY MANCINI

MY HEART WILL GO ON

(Love Theme from 'Titanic')

from the Paramount and Twentieth Century Fox Motion Picture TITANIC

VIOLIN

Music by JAMES HORNER
Lyric by WILL JENNINGS

OVER THE RAINBOW

from THE WIZARD OF OZ

VIOLIN

Music by HAROLD ARLEN
Lyric by E.Y. "YIP" HARBURG

PIANO MAN

VIOLIN

Words and Music by
BILLY JOEL

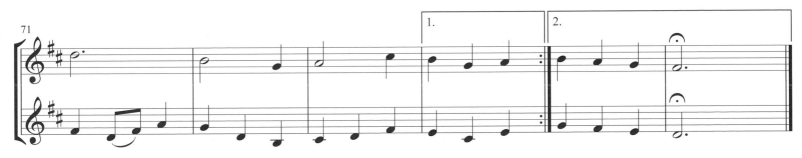

(Sittin' On)
THE DOCK OF THE BAY

VIOLIN

Words and Music by STEVE CROPPER
and OTIS REDDING

CODA

D.S. al Coda

SMELLS LIKE TEEN SPIRIT

VIOLIN

Words and Music by KURT COBAIN,
KRIST NOVOSELIC and DAVE GROHL

STAND BY ME

VIOLIN

Words and Music by JERRY LEIBER,
MIKE STOLLER and BEN E. KING

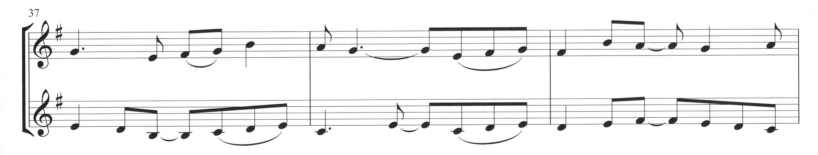

TEARS IN HEAVEN

VIOLIN

Words and Music by ERIC CLAPTON
and WILL JENNINGS

UNCHAINED MELODY

VIOLIN

Lyric by HY ZARET
Music by ALEX NORTH

WHAT A WONDERFUL WORLD

VIOLIN

Words and Music by GEORGE DAVID WEISS
and BOB THIELE

WHAT THE WORLD NEEDS NOW IS LOVE

VIOLIN

Lyric by HAL DAVID
Music by BURT BACHARACH

Slow Jazz Waltz

To Coda

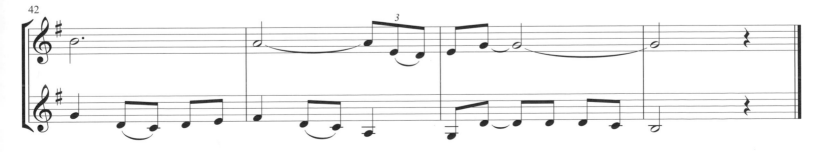

A WHITER SHADE OF PALE

VIOLIN

Words and Music by KEITH REID,
GARY BROOKER and MATTHEW FISHER

WITH OR WITHOUT YOU

VIOLIN

Words and Music by
U2

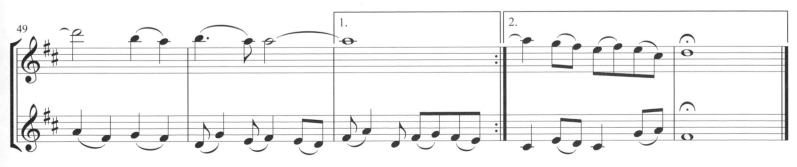

YOU RAISE ME UP

VIOLIN

Words and Music by BRENDAN GRAHAM
and ROLF LOVLAND

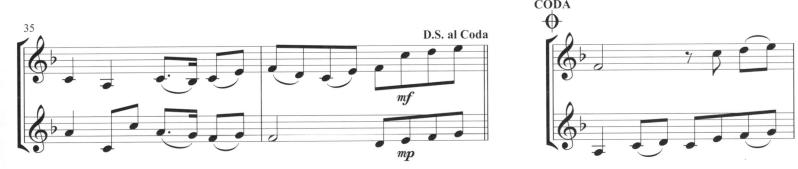

YOU'VE LOST THAT LOVIN' FEELIN'

VIOLIN

Words and Music by BARRY MANN,
CYNTHIA WEIL and PHIL SPECTOR

Slow and steady

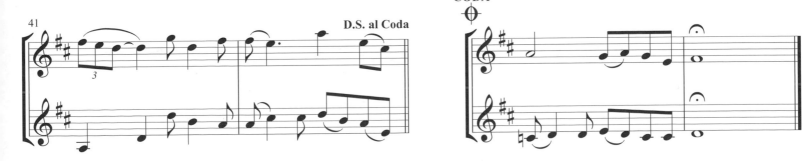

YOUR SONG

VIOLIN

Words and Music by ELTON JOHN
and BERNIE TAUPIN

Moderate Ballad, in 2

VIOLIN DUET
COLLECTIONS

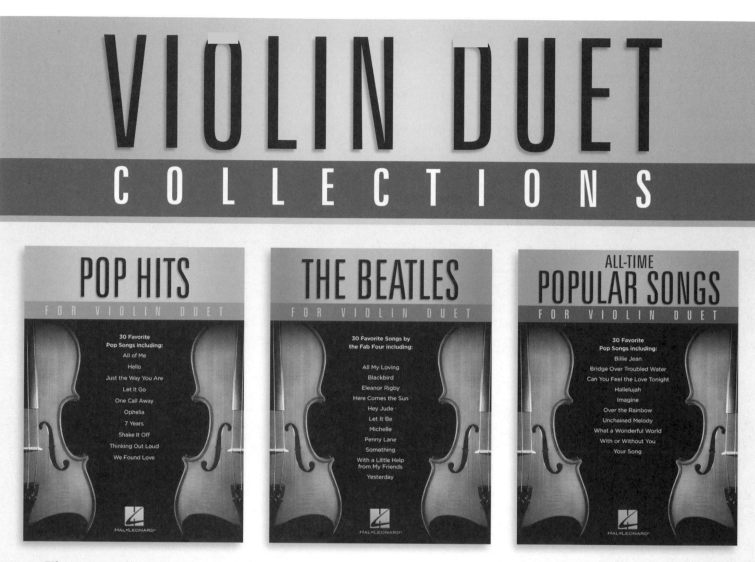

These collections are designed for violinists familiar with first position and comfortable reading basic rhythms. Each two-page arrangement includes a violin 1 and violin 2 part, with each taking a turn at playing the melody for a fun and challenging ensemble experience.

ALL-TIME POPULAR SONGS FOR VIOLIN DUET

Billie Jean • Bridge over Troubled Water • Can You Feel the Love Tonight • Hallelujah • Imagine • Over the Rainbow • Unchained Melody • What a Wonderful World • With or Without You • Your Song and more.

00222449 . . . . $14.99

THE BEATLES FOR VIOLIN DUET

All My Loving • Blackbird • Eleanor Rigby • A Hard Day's Night • Hey Jude • Let It Be • Michelle • Ob-La-Di, Ob-La-Da • Something • When I'm Sixty-Four • Yesterday and more.

00218245 . . . . $14.99

POP HITS FOR VIOLIN DUET

All of Me • Hello • Just the Way You Are • Let It Go • Love Yourself • Ophelia • Riptide • Say Something • Shake It Off • Story of My Life • Take Me to Church • Thinking Out Loud • Wake Me Up! and more.

00217577 . . . . $14.99

DISNEY SONGS FOR VIOLIN DUET

Beauty and the Beast • Can You Feel the Love Tonight • Colors of the Wind • Do You Want to Build a Snowman? • Hakuna Matata • How Far I'll Go • I'm Wishing • Let It Go • Some Day My Prince Will Come • A Spoonful of Sugar • Under the Sea • When She Loved Me • A Whole New World and more.

00217578 . . . . $14.99

HAL•LEONARD®
www.halleonard.com

Prices, contents, and availability subject to change without notice.